Graveyard Love

Lisa Marie Roby

authorHOUSE®

AuthorHouse™
1663 Liberty Drive
Bloomington, IN 47403
www.authorhouse.com
Phone: 1-800-839-8640

© 2012 by Lisa Marie Roby. All rights reserved.

No part of this book may be reproduced, stored in a retrieval system, or transmitted by any means without the written permission of the author.

First published by AuthorHouse   12/30/2011

ISBN: 978-1-4685-3928-8 (sc)
ISBN: 978-1-4685-3927-1 (ebk)

Library of Congress Control Number: 2012900005

Printed in the United States of America

Any people depicted in stock imagery provided by Thinkstock are models, and such images are being used for illustrative purposes only.
Certain stock imagery © Thinkstock.

Because of the dynamic nature of the Internet, any web addresses or links contained in this book may have changed since publication and may no longer be valid. The views expressed in this work are solely those of the author and do not necessarily reflect the views of the publisher, and the publisher hereby disclaims any responsibility for them.

Table of Contents
(Chapters by Titles)

A Taste of My Life (Bittersweet), 1
Darkest Before Day, 12
Face to Face, 18

Who's to Blame?, 20
Do I Live or Do I Die? (That's the Question), 23
Unending Pain or Longsuffering, 25
The Pains of Facing Fear, 29

A New Day, 31
Unraveling, 33
Bits and Pieces, 36
Weeping May Endure for a Night . . . But Joy's Coming In the Morning, 38

Unbelievable, 40
Healing My Way, 42
Victim or Criminal, 44
From The Skillet to the Frying Pan, 46

Can't Win For Losing, 52
Help Is On the Way, 55
Joy Comes From Within, 58
The Prayer Line, 61

Taking My Life Back, 65
Letting Go and Letting God, 68
Harvesting New Life, 70

Saying Good-Bye to Daddy, 75
My Latter Will Be Greater, 77

Letter to Mother, 81
Letter to Father, 83

About the Editor, 85
About the Author, 87

GraveYard Love

"Set me as a seal upon thine heart, as a seal upon thine arm: For love is strong as death; jealously is cruel as the grave: The coals thereof are coals of fire, which hath a most vehement flame."
Song of Solomon 8:6

Non-Fiction written by
Lisa M. Roby

Dedication

I would like to dedicate this book to God, my Father, Jesus, my Savior, and the Holy Ghost, my keeper. I thank God, the Creator of all, for being present throughout every encounter in my life. You have kept me sane through the most difficult times in my life. Nobody but you could have kept my mind in total peace!! I would also like to give special thanks to my Savior, Jesus Christ, for loving me enough to come to earth to be the living example, the living Word of God and most of all for being my intercessor then and now. Thank you for teaching me through life experiences to love and forgive others as well as myself. I thank God for giving me an opportunity to write this book in order to share with others my experiences have made me what I am today. I realize that it was important to write this book with elegance, style, grace, patience and love under your direction.

In Loving Memory of my Mom and Dad

Preface

As an editor I worked with the author to gather information that formulated this book I considered how important it was for me to feel the emotions and understand the roles discussed within this book as much as possible. I physically traveled to places that I had never been before. Well, putting someone else's thoughts into words entail more unspoken details that must find there way onto the paper in rare form which is one reason I decided not to tamper with the vernacular of the characters within this book. Details became my best friend as I listened to the past speak out its story to me. I visited old living quarters, cemeteries, abandoned houses almost a century old and every site had a different story to tell that I never knew existed. The literature you are about to experience was written not only by the author but also by her past that is very much alive in her. In all my experiences with reading varieties of books this is the first time I could hear the author's past scream from the core of the earth for me to hear her right now and write her story.

This piece of literature was mind blowing as I felt obligated to actually apply its lessons within my own life—Forgiveness. Editing the material within this book took on a life of its own. Writing about forgiveness gave me the opportunity to walk through the author's life page by page feeling the hurts and disappointments, joys, and successes I always enjoy in works of other authors. I have been enlightened by the truths and the horrific details of the experiences within this piece of literature; as I indeed believe and hope each reader will experience as well. I only ask that you open your hearts and minds to receive every opportunity to grow from another person's life experiences so that the author's pain will not be in vain. Each individual person within this universe was made to endure something, which is why we share the joys and pains of each other's lives so that growth can take place in an individual's life in every possible way. Just as babies grow physically, adults continue to develop internally by inviting another person's experience that can elevate us within our very own world without having to repeat history.

It has been a pleasure working with the author of this book, Mrs. Lisa Roby as we worked together to complete this piece of literature. We were friends before ever working together on this project and I must say working together has given me a new respect for our friendship. I appreciate the opportunity she has given me to expand my horizons within the editing world during this project. I am very thankful for Mrs. Roby's trust that she has in me to put her life into words for others to use as a guide to live by. You are to be commended greatly, Lisa, for thinking of God's people in such a mighty way by sharing your own story. It has been my lifelong dream to write and edit a book of this nature and now I know this is just the beginning of many books to come for me, too. Thank you, Lisa for believing in me and trusting me to get done the job you assigned me to do! I love you, Sis.

1

A Taste of My Life (Bittersweet)

I was born in 1968, I lived on a Plantation in Arkansas. That's right on a plantation. It was a plantation not so different from what you may have heard about or seen on television or maybe even read about in textbooks. My family had most of what we needed to get by on the plantation for the most part—food and work. Unlike most Black folks during the 1960's that had large families, I grew up an only child with my momma and daddy. I was a fortunate child true enough to have both momma and daddy living together under one roof but during those days many of us were fortunate all the same. My parents were my best friends as I grew up. I remember my momma being like my big sister; we could even wear each other's clothes and shoes (my mama was a very petite lady). Most of the time things were good in our home between momma and daddy at which time *I* was the happiest. But there were times when things didn't go so well. I can recall a time when we didn't have enough money, work or food so momma sent me to live with my daddy's momma for a while. I went there 'cause she lived the closest to us.

My daddy was a sharecropper by trade and unfortunately crops were sparse more often than not. But I was able to go back home when there was ample food; of course, that meant work was good and money plenteous for our small family.

Despite all the bad times, I enjoyed being home with my momma and daddy more than anything. I love them both so very much. Sometimes I felt I could be just as happy at home when we did not have enough as long as I was with them.

As an only child I got bored a lot. I can remember complaining to my momma about needing someone my own age to play with and how I wished that I had somebody to do kid stuff with sometime. I didn't want to hurt her feelings so I said it in the best way I knew how as a child could. You see Momma wanted to be everything to me and indeed she was. She would always try to make a bad situation better so one day she gave me the cutest, bright—eyed puppy that I named Brownie. Brownie was the beginning of my ongoing love I have for animals. Soon after Brownie came along I momma got me a kitten, too; I called her Kitty. *I don't know why I never came up with a better name for Kitty.* Momma didn't know which I liked best so she got both for me since *she* wanted me to be happy. Momma and daddy didn't have to see my long face any more after those two came along. I did a good job of taking care of them, too. I fed them, bathed them and played with them outside. Although the animals kept me busy most of the time, I would notice both my parents starting to drink more than their usual share on weekends. They started to drink until they each got sloppy drunk. Drunken behavior was not uncommon when they were at parties or had friends over but the every other day drinking with no other friends around them caught my attention fast. My parents didn't just get drunk and pass out like some people do, but they got drunk to argue and fight with each other. I hated to see two people who loved each other act out so awful. It was as though they liked each other better when they got drunk though 'cause at least they were talking to each other then. They did not communicate much when they were sober but boy they make up for lost time after a few drinks. Soon those arguments grew into fistfights and everything changed in our happy little family. I hated so much to see my parents drinking 'cause I knew what was coming up next.

Momma and daddy started to fight so much that I started running off to the neighbor's house. I remember choosing the Henry's house to run to. I could get to the Henry's fast. Whenever I knocked on the door to their house I would be in tears and just plain out of breathe but always in my pajamas. They would allow me wash my face and would give me something to eat to take my mind off of my troubles. I knew what they were trying to do and it worked every time. I started knocking on the Henry's door so often until they would have a plate in the refrigerator all ready wrapped and waiting for me. The Henry's knew from the first time that I showed up at their house what was going on at my house and allowed me to stay as long as I needed to with no questions asked.

One night I could hear my daddy calling my name from down the street as I sat enjoying a hot plate of food at the Henry's. My heart started to beat so hard I thought my chest would burst wide open. You see, daddy had told me to stop running off to the neighbor's house because that puts other people in his family's business but I didn't listen to him 'cause I felt like if he wanted me to stop running to the neighbors then he and momma should stop fighting. This one particular night when daddy got to Mr. Henry's property, he found me there safe inside as he would always and said, "Come on let's go home," as he always did as if he had given me permission to be there. Well on the way home as we were walking down the road, my daddy started beating me with his belt in the middle of the street and yelled, "Haven't I told you about running off from home?" Too hurt to respond, I just nodded my head with tears rolling down my freshly washed face only to make *new* tear streaks to wipe away on my own this time. The minute I got home I went into my room and only cried harder, but silently because I didn't want another beating. Unfortunately, these types of scenarios went on for many more years to come. On the outside my parents appeared to be two very normal people who loved each other and they did when they were sober. Momma was a soft-spoken lady with a small and fragile frame but, wow, did she have a big heart to do for others. She spent all of her life doing things for other people not just working to get money either; and not once did I ever hear her complain about anything she ever did even when the favors were never returned. Daddy on the other hand stood over 6 feet tall and was anything but quiet—he would tell you exactly how he felt; but he was a kind person most of the time. I believed both my parents loved me because they always supported me by showing up at school events or any other activities that interested me; they seemed to forget me only when they drank too much.

Overall, daddy was a good provider. He worked hard as a sharecropper tilling other people's land five days a week and sometimes six days. Momma worked mostly during the summer months but was home with me most of her time. She was a wonderful mother. She was a woman of high moral character and was excellent at her duties as a wife and mother.

No one could say that momma, Martha, wasn't taking care of her family. She took care of us whether she had a job to go to or not. She paid bills when daddy could give her money; she cooked, cleaned, ironed and even cut the grass. I watched as momma would run daddy's bath water and do anything else that she thought he needed or wanted done. Although momma treated daddy like a king, he was still unfaithful to her and she knew it, too. Momma didn't complain about that either; as a matter of fact, she never even mentioned it. But everybody knew what was going on even I knew just from the way he treated momma that he was happier someplace else. He just didn't want to leave momma and me so instead we got the energy he had left from his day. *I suppose that was morality for him—not kicking us to the curb.*

Mom could always tell when I was thinking too hard about something 'cause she would always say something funny or child-like to get my attention to take my mind off whatever was on it. One time I was in deep thought about a fight momma and daddy had gotten into and she walked over to the front window of the house, looked out and said, "Come here baby, Ain't that a nice mower Mr. Henry got but look how his butt sticks out while he pushing it; it makes cutting the grass look so easy don't it?" Of course, I agreed and we laughed and laughed about that until I found myself in a conversation with momma that took my mind right off momma and daddy's fight I kept thinking of. Nonetheless, my parents' often fought so violently that it would take more than Mr. Henry's wonderful lawn mower to take my mind off it. I'm reminded of a time momma and daddy had a terrible fight. I can't remember what it was about but daddy had been out of town and naturally momma was glad to see him. I was glad mostly 'cause momma was glad. Momma said to daddy, "Are you hungry? Let me fix you something to eat." I don't recall him daddy responding but she was just that eager to do something nice for him. So she went into the kitchen to fix him a plate of pork-chops with some biscuits and gravy. She walked ever so gracefully as she served him the plate of food. I stayed in the kitchen while momma took daddy his plate—I was so proud of my momma. I remember saying to myself, *"I want to do the same things for my husband one day."* The next thing I heard was a crash and then a loud scream. I ran as fast as I could to see what happened. When I got to the other room all I could see was the blood rushing from my momma's head and my daddy walking out the front door. I watched him walk away from the damage he had done from the same window momma and I laughed at Mr. Henry from earlier that day. I knew then it was up to me to get help for momma. We didn't have a phone, so I grabbed my momma and lifted her over my back and walked as fast as a 10year old could while carrying her momma. Momma's blood ran down to my feet leaving a trail from our front door to the neighbor's door. God and His angels helped me to carry momma that night. I had to walk two houses down to get to neighbors with a car and a phone. I kicked on the door and screamed, "Somebody help me,

please!" while I used the rest of my body to hold momma. The neighbor finally came to the door, but by then momma was out cold. I thought she was dead so I started screaming hysterically. The neighbor was able to calm me by saying, "Your momma is breathing let's get her in the car." The neighbors drove to the County Hospital while I explained what happened. I remember praying to God, *"Please don't let my momma die and thank You for helping me to carry momma to some help."* The nurse at the hospital was able to bandage momma's head and the doctor told her that one more inch of that plate into her skull and that would have been her death. Since this was a domestic violence incident the hospital had to notify authorities. I was happy about that but I kept that piece of information to myself. I figured since the police had to get involved that would make momma and daddy stop fighting. The police officer came over to speak to momma and asked, "Would you like to press charges, Ma'am?" momma replied "No Sir." and right then my hope for peace seemed to disappear right out the hospital doors. The police officer expressed to momma how lucky he thought she was to still be alive.

That night my momma and I stayed at Grandma's house (momma's momma). That didn't last long because daddy knew momma didn't have anywhere else to go but back to her parents' house. He showed up to get us and took momma and me right on back home. Daddy cried and apologized the whole ride home. He apologized for what he had done and said that it would never happen again. Momma never exchanged words or complained about that either or brought up that incident again—not even once. Shortly after that incident daddy moved us to Hughes, Arkansas. Hughes wasn't far from at all from Bruins where we were from but it was a change; although, I didn't like it much when we got there. We had to use an outhouse because there was no indoor plumbing. We also had to pump our own water and use a stove that stood in the middle of the living room. I thought that when people moved from one place to another it's because they found something better not worse. In Hughes, I had to walk down a long dirt road to get to my bus stop for school only to be the first one on the bus and the last one off everyday. On my way to the bus stop I would stop at the neighborhood candy lady to buy candy and cookies; this was the highlight of my day except when I didn't have any money.

My momma's parents were school janitors at the town's elementary and high schools; granddaddy was the janitor during the entire time I attended the elementary school. I enjoyed being around my granddaddy; especially, when he would come to our house to help momma clean fish for us to eat. He would spend hours at a time with us and have talks with momma about her drinking so much, too. He would tell her that she and my daddy wouldn't fight so much if *she* would stop drinking because you can't change nobody but yourself.

> *"God grant me the serenity to accept the things I cannot change, Courage to change the things I can and wisdom to know the difference." (Author Unknown)*

I loved being around my grandparents and other elderly people because they spoke words that just felt good to my soul—truth. My grandparents and their friends would always tell me that I have seen too much for a child my age. God gave me premature wisdom I say. I have to admit I liked to hear them talk about me like that, so long as they were talking to me and with me. It only made me want to hear more of what they had to say regardless of who or what it was about. I learned a lot around my momma and grandma. I learned how to do everything momma did around the house including write out checks to pay bills and how to mail them.

It was here in Hughes that I noticed my momma drinking more and more during the weekdays and not just on weekends. I would find empty bottles hidden in the drawers of my room where momma was hiding them from my daddy. I found myself protecting her drunkenness from him, too. When momma would walk down the hall and stagger, I would quickly get behind her so that daddy wouldn't notice it. I love momma and daddy and would do anything to keep them from arguing at all cost to me.

On one occasion my parents had a birthday party for my Grandma at our house. I got very excited because I got to see relatives that I don't see all of the time. That night I hated to see everyone leaving although one of my cousins was staying overnight with us. I started feeling like something bad was going to happen 'cause we were having too much fun. After everyone left that night my daddy didn't take long to start arguing with my momma. Daddy hit momma almost immediately after the last guest stepped out the door. Surprisingly, my cousin jumped on daddy's back and I decided to help her so I started hitting my daddy with my fist and yelling for him to stop hitting on momma all the time. Daddy turned and slapped me so hard that I hit the floor and he then took off his belt and commenced to beat my cousin's butt and mine for butting into grown folks business. My momma told me that I had no right to treat my daddy that way and to apologize to him immediately. I told momma, *"yes Ma'am I will; I'm just tired of him beating on you is all."* I felt like my hands had been tied behind my back especially, now that I'm not supposed to retaliate.

*"Do not say, "I'll do to him as he has done to me; I'll pay that man back for what he did." * (NKJV Proverbs 24:29)

Soon I started acting out by failing the third grade. I stayed to myself most of the time because I didn't want anyone to know about the fighting that went on in my house. I started to withdraw from the neighborhood friends I had—I would not go outside to play. I was completely withdrawn.

In time, I met a girl named Linda and we became friends. Linda was like me and didn't have many friends either. Linda's excuse was different from mine because her parents were 'sanctified' and believed girls should wear nothing but dresses all the time. So her parents made *her* wear dresses everyday—long dresses. Linda was the only girl I knew who had to wear dresses all the time. Linda's dresses didn't bother me though 'cause she was friendly. She was real nice to me and I wasn't afraid to be myself around her. She even invited me to visit her church. I usually attended church with my grandma at Walnut Grove Baptist Church. My momma chose a different denomination to worship with—the Jehovah's Witness. The Witnesses weren't like grandma's church friends. Momma remained with them until the members learned that she smoked cigarettes and they put her out of the Kingdom Hall. Kingdom Hall is what the Witnesses call their temple. Shortly after the Witnesses put momma out, she joined Bright Star Baptist Church. I did not become a member there either. I only wanted to be at my grandma's church where I was most comfortable. My friend Linda and I realized that we could hang out together more if I could visit her church because then I would get to spend the entire week-end at her parents' house; we lived too far to walk to visit each other. My parents and grandparents felt it was a good idea for me to visit other churches. So when Linda invited me to come along with her to church momma said it was okay. Linda was a member of a holiness church. It was a small church. The preacher acknowledged my presence although I was only 11years old at the time. I had never visited a holiness church before I met Linda. I was fascinated to see how sanctified people worshipped God. I heard people shouting loud praises to God, dancing all around the building, singing and testifying. I really liked that because it made me feel welcomed and loved—like one of the family. I was so glad that my parents allowed me to visit with Linda and her family. Whenever I attended Linda's church I would stay the entire weekend with Linda and her family. Linda's parents were just as kind to me at their home as the church members were to me. They treated me like I was their daughter. I would always pack dresses to wear while I was at their house mainly because I knew Linda would be wearing them, too. After my first visit to Linda's church, I started reading my Bible all of the time, praying more, and wearing dresses most of the time. Reading and praying seemed to comfort my spirit making me like myself more; even though, lots of other children seemed to dislike Linda and me because of our differences from them. I also made sure I was more obedient to my parents and grandparents because Linda's pastor stressed children obeying their parents every time I visited like he knew I wasn't listening to my parents or something.

2

Darkest Before Day

My momma was born a twin, Martha and Mary. Martha was my momma and Mary died shortly after childbirth so I never got a chance to know her. My momma's parents had a large family; I had cousins that I didn't even know. I didn't spend a lot of time with my momma's side of the family then or now for that matter. However, I spent plenty of time with my daddy's side of the family. We knew each other real well. It was easier for me to be with my daddy's family because they knew about the abuse that my momma endured so I didn't have to act like everything was fine around them.

It was March 4, 1984, I was 15 years old at the time. I awoke to get dressed for school as I normally did. My momma called out to me, "Child do you feel well?" I told her that I just had a weird feeling that made me uneasy in my stomach. Momma didn't usually call on me the way she did this particular morning, but she felt the same as I did this day. So, of course, I continued getting dressed for school and afterwards went out to catch the school bus. While I was on the bus I tried to take my mind off the funny feeling inside so I started thinking about how calm things had been with my parents and how glad I was about that. I suddenly started feeling like I just wanted to give my momma the biggest hug I could give her. The entire day at school was just as it was on the bus—weird. I started feeling impatient to get home. During school I ran into my grandma as she worked cleaning the girl's bathroom. When she saw me she called my name—"Lisa, come here. Are you alright 'cause you just standing there like your mind is a million miles away." "Aw, h*ey grandma. Naw, I've been feeling weird all morning and it just won't go away no matter how much I try to concentrate on something else. Instead of getting better this feeling just gets worse and stronger, "I replied.* "That's funny 'cause I been feeling the same strangeness, too. Don't worry to much though, 'cause whatever it is, it's gonna be alright." Later when the school bus finally got to my stop on the way home, I ran all the way to my house-yelling hey to neighbors as I ran by. I dropped my books as soon as I stepped foot inside the house and called out for momma. When I saw her I gave her that big hug that I thought about while riding the bus. I told her that I loved her very much and about my weird feelings I had all that day. Later that evening momma gave me $30 because she had gotten her income taxes back from the government. I was so happy to get any money that my momma gave me. Momma asked me to drive her to the store where she bought beer and cigarettes. I wasn't' happy about what she bought but I was still happy just to be with my momma.

The neighbors had invited my parents over earlier in the week to play cards so they took me along with them. I played with the children in the backyard and then inside the house. I could hear the adults in the other room talking loud and cussing casually at each other. I just sat there wondering how the children could ignore the adults so well. Some time passed when I heard my momma asking daddy if he was ready to leave to go home, but daddy told her to go on without him. So then momma called for me to leave with her and we got in the car and went home. All the way home I had that weird feeling in my stomach again. When we got home I told my momma I had a weird feeling that when daddy gets home he is going to start a fight with her. But momma just said, "Your daddy ain't going to hurt nobody." So I just tried to ignore my feelings like the neighbor's children ignored the adults yelling and cussing at each other. Instead of going to sleep, I sat on the couch waiting on my daddy to come home. I was used to staying awake in my bed until I knew daddy was home and asleep.

The window next to the couch was opened and I could hear daddy getting out of the neighbor's car while they dropped him off at home. As soon as daddy walked into the house he started by asking me how much money my momma had given me earlier that day. I told him that momma had given me $30 and that was all. As I took the money out my drawer daddy snatched it from me before I could unfold it.

Daddy asked, "Where is your momma?" I told him that she was in the kitchen but then he shouted, "When I get out of the bathroom both of you B . . . s better be gone." I started to walk toward the dinning room and glanced into the bathroom where my daddy was standing and he looked like somebody else to me. Daddy's face was darker and angrier than I had ever seen it and his eyes were red like fire. I walked faster toward the kitchen where momma was to persuade her that we should just leave and let daddy cool off tonight. But before momma could make a decision to leave the house daddy stood at the kitchen door with a shotgun in front of momma and me. Daddy asked momma if she was reaching for a knife as he pointed the gun at her? Momma reassured him that she was not reaching for a knife and asked him not to point that shotgun at her. Daddy continued pointing the shotgun at momma though; momma's words or the calmness in her voice did not move him at all to back down. Momma then said, "Shoot me then m . . .!" I wanted so badly to do something to make daddy stop acting so this way. I mean why was he doing this. *Was a shotgun really necessary?* I looked at the kitchen table and spotted the iron, I wanted to grab it to hit him but for some reason I could not move my body. I tried but my arms and legs wouldn't budge. All of a sudden the shotgun sounded, "Boom!" Daddy stood still aimed at my momma's tiny little feet but missed, thank God. The force of that bullet left a large hole in the kitchen floor. I yelled and screamed for daddy to please stop. I yelled, "Daddy, why you doing this?!" Daddy was determined to shoot momma. He yelled at me and said, "Shut up, girl, you don't know nothing about this now move out the way!" Daddy walked toward the back door and as he did I got up and ran to stand in front of my momma. She tried pushing me out of the way but I yelled to daddy, "If you want to shoot somebody then shoot me. I will die for momma 'cause she is all I got!" Daddy looked as though he would take me up on the offer for a minute but then he walked over and grabbed my momma by the arm and pushed her down on the couch. She cried telling me to run next door for help and surprisingly daddy just watched as I backed out of the door. Once I was out of the door I ran as fast as I could to get help. In the meantime, I could still hear my momma pleading with my daddy not to do this. I had made it to the neighbor's house.

15

I put one foot on the first step to go up to the front door and **"BOOM!"** The shotgun went off and I dropped to my knees right on the neighbor's steps and screamed, "No, No, No! He shot my momma!" Then the neighbors ran over to my parent's house to see what all the commotion was about. My neighbor ran past me yelling for me to go inside their house and close the door. So I did. A few minutes later I heard that same neighbor cranking their car and pulling out of the driveway heading toward my parent's house again.

A police officer whose name we'll call Smitt just happened to live up the street from us. I ran out of the house toward officer Smitt's house crying nervously to tell him what happened. Meanwhile, the neighbors were passing by in their car and I turned and saw my daddy in the car with them. I immediately ran down to hide in a nearby ditch so that daddy couldn't see me. The car began to slow down and came to a stop in front of Smitt's house and my dad got out of the car. While daddy walked up to Smitt's door, I sneaked from the ditch to the neighbor's car to get inside to be with momma. The neighbors locked the doors and told me to get away from the car and go back to their house and wait there. I overheard daddy talking to Smitt about his wife who had been shot and that he would like an escort to the hospital if possible. Smitt was unable to give them an escort to the hospital but relieved them of any worries while getting her there.

The next thing I knew was that my grandma (daddy's momma) and my momma's brother were driving up. I never saw grandma move so fast. Grandma saw the police approaching me I guess because by the time she got to me she answered the police before I could hear the question. Grandma said, "You wait 'til later to ask her any questions." I told grandma that I was able to answer questions now because I could only answer what I knew. I walked with the police over to his car where I was allowed to sit and talk to him. While I sat in the police car I watched other officers going in and out of our house some with yellow tape and some with cameras. Somehow I managed to answer the few questions that the police asked me. Afterwards the policeman opened the car door for me and I noticed my whole body just felt numb. *Is this the cause of my weird feelings all day long? God, were you trying to tell me that all of this was going to happen to us today?* The officer said he was going back in the house to help gather evidence. He asked me was I going to be all right here alone. I replied, "I guess so." *I am so afraid daddy is coming back to get me, too. God, why was it my momma? I told you I would die for her. I would have given my life for my momma. She was a wonderful woman. She did not deserve to be hurt; especially by someone who claimed to love her.* The police officer finally came back to the car and took me to my maternal grandma's house. Grandma was at the door of the house waiting for me when we pulled up in her driveway. I could tell that she had been crying when I walked up to her. She hugged me and told me to come on in and sit down. When I sat down grandma sat down beside me. She said, "Child, your mother didn't make it. She was shot in the back. She's gone, baby; it's a loss for both of us." I immediately started screaming to the top of my voice; I felt like I was about to loose my mind. Grandma tried to hold me down. We both held each other and cried and cried and cried. I wanted my momma back—to see her, to hug her, to smell her and to see her tiny little feet *moving* around again.

3

Face to Face

I had not slept since the night before my momma was shot. Grandma cooked most of my favorite foods but I still couldn't eat. I spent most of my time inside the house sitting in the fetal position. *What was I to do now—with my momma dead and my daddy in prison? What about me? Who's gonna take care of me? I wish daddy had thought about what would happen to me?* I spent several of days wearing the same clothes at my grandma's house after she broke the news to me about my momma. I overheard grandma on the telephone making funeral arrangements and saying that she would take me to my parent's house to pick up some of my things. I longed to go back to the house where my momma spent her last moments. I remember looking back as I ran for help and seeing her watch me from the window inside the house. I looked back just to let her know that I was hurrying to get help as fast as I could. Grandma came into the room where I was as she had done for the past few days—quietly as if not to disturb me. But this time she sat on the bed and explained to me that we needed to make a trip to my parent's house and that "things ain't been cleaned up yet." Grandma wanted to know if I would be all right going inside the house not knowing what I might see. I moved from my fetal position and asked her when do we leave? I thought to myself, *"I finally get to feel momma again."* When grandma and I arrived at my parent's house the first thing I spotted was blood on the ground and on the sides of the front porch. We walked up the steps to the door and saw dried blood on it, too. Grandma said, "Girl, you all right, you can wait in the car if you want to?" I just nodded and kept walking up the porch steps to the front door. I walked into the house and right where momma stood looking out of the window was a puddle of blood. The blood was all dried up around the edges but toward the center of the puddle was real dark, cold and wet. *Momma didn't fight back at all, she just let daddy take her life from her—from me.* As I stood there looking at the blood I felt the saliva come alive in my mouth. Just then I covered my mouth trying to hold back the feeling to vomit and grandma put her arm around me and walked with me toward my bedroom but I threw up along the way. I just lost it completely from the inside out. I felt my life leaving my body because of the overwhelming feelings of hurt. I sat in a room toward the back of the house and grandma gathered my things together in a bag for me. While I sat waiting on grandma I could hear more relatives come into the house saying, "I'm gonna take this lamp right here and these pictures." I was too numb to respond at the time. One of them came into the room where I sat and didn't bother to ask how I was feeling or what she could do but she said, "You want to take something with you that belong to your momma." I looked up and answered, "No." Those relatives that came to the house that day took whatever they could without a second thought about what had just happened to my life.

4

Who's to Blame?

I grew angry with everybody—momma, daddy, my grandparents, God and myself; there had to be somebody I could blame for momma's death other than my daddy. Somebody must have seen this horrible fate coming—grandma, neighbors, and friends. *I mean really, how many violent episodes did my parents have to have before the grand finale?* I was left with nothing—financially, emotionally and spiritually. Everyday after momma's death I faced new problems. My grandma didn't know how we were going to pay for momma's funeral or even just a proper burial. Daddy couldn't help with it being in jail and all. *Not like anyone would welcome his help anyway.* Grandma prayed aloud one day while asking God to see us through this awful ordeal. Nevertheless, I considered a small detail from the day momma gave me the $30 from her taxes before she died. I noticed an envelope in her hand that day as she stopped along the way by the mailbox and dropped the envelope inside. The envelope was addressed to an insurance company. *It was not uncommon for me to notice small details about momma's "grown folk business."* I'm so glad I did notice the envelope that day because that information gave grandma confirmation that God would answer her prayer. Because of that envelope momma mailed, (which happened to be an insurance payment), Grandma was able to give momma a decent funeral service and a proper burial. The funeral was nice but lasted grossly too long. *It's amazing how people you haven't seen in ages come out of nowhere just to have something to say about someone they hardly ever visited or called. I don't want anyone speaking about me at my funeral that was not an ongoing part of my life before I die and I mean that too.* Before the funeral grandma gave the mortician momma's usher uniform that she wore at church to be used as her final resting garments. *Maybe momma will be waiting in heaven to usher me in one day.* Once all the talking was over and when everyone was done viewing momma's tiny little frame in that big beautiful casket that *she* bought, then the immediate family had a chance to view her body. When my turn came around to view momma I just kept starring at how peaceful she looked to me. It looked like she was floating between cloud angels that held her tiny body ever so gently. It still didn't matter about how peaceful she may have looked I still wanted my momma back, alive moving around and with me as she always had been. I did not want that day to be the last day that I would lay eyes on her.

There had been a time when I was afraid to see a hearse drive by before my momma had to be hosted in one but after she died I would look for them as though I was closer to her when I could lay my eyes on one. "All of the arguing, fussing and fighting was all over for momma now and I still can't be happy about it," I said aloud to myself. I was so mad at momma but pitied her and longed for her all at the same time. My emotional roller coaster ride was starting to get out of hand. The feelings that turned my stomach would not easily go away and when they did they always showed up again unannounced.

I was stricken with emotions that made me **want** to think hard about every detail of that horrible day—*How was she dressed? Did she say anything earlier that should have let me know that she would die that day? Did daddy show signs that he would finally . . .?* I had to think about details; I wanted to think and made myself think over and over again until I would eventually fall asleep. This behavior of mine went on for months.

After the funeral I lived with my momma's parents. I got to their house with the few things that I wanted to salvage from my parents house and the memories of my shattered life. I would try thinking of good times like when my parents weren't drinking and arguing with each other or about my dog, Brownie, and Kitty, my cat; to get the ringing sound of the fatal gunshot out of my head but the shotgun would sound off in the middle my pleasant memories, too. I didn't have any peace in my mind. As much as I liked going to church I stopped going because I blamed God so much for taking my momma when He knew darn well that I needed my momma. *Christ, don't all girls need their momma?*

Didn't He think about me being a girl and how many questions I would have for my momma one day? Did He care about that? Why couldn't He just have taken me?

5

Do I Live or Do I Die? (That's the Question)

I was almost sixteen years old and so much had gone on in my life. Time had come for me return to school. I had been out for several weeks. My grades were already suffering before momma died because of the constant fights my parents had. I really didn't try much after momma died. *Why should I? Who would care? Do grandma and granddaddy really care or do they have to act like they do because they know I don't have anyone else to turn to?* While I was walking home from school one day I started thinking about how much I hated my life now. *I love my grandparents but I don't want to live with them I want my momma!*

On my way back, I decided to take a different route home this particular day so that I would walk over the bridge. I walked toward the ramp of the bridge, stepped up on top of it, stood there and contemplated jumping off. I stood up straight and I could feel fear but not enough to make me come down on my own and just as I had made up my mind to jump my cousin came out of nowhere and pulled me backwards off the ramp. "Girl, what's the matter with you?" she said to me. She really did come out of nowhere. That was my first suicide attempt. My cousin continued talking to me about how much I had to live for as we walked back toward my grandparents' house. *I couldn't see that I had anything else to live for.* Later that next week I was thinking about killing myself again. This time I would find a way to be private about it; so I decided that overdosing on pills would be just the thing. The only pills that I found at the time were aspirin and decided they would have to do. Well, when I took them I had a really bad stomachache, nausea and vomiting but death was nowhere to be found. I mean death wouldn't even answer my phone calls. I was too embarrassed at the time to tell anyone about that failed attempt.

After the second attempt of suicide didn't work I decided to start talking to my friends at my school about the how important it is to listen to their parents and to let their parents know just how much they love and appreciate them. I would also tell them to never wish death on anyone no matter how mad they make you because one day death will visit that person not because you wished it on them but because it is a part of life and you don't want to spend the rest of your life feeling guilty while thinking their death was your fault. I just wanted my friends to enjoy their life with their family. Most of my friends seemed to be so happy at school and at home from my point of view and I didn't want them to allow anything to wreck their happiness. And no matter who can do for you the things that your parents can do, you will never get another mother or father after they are gone. I just wanted everybody to realize that and to remember those words during this time in my life.

6

Unending Pain or Longsuffering

It was my junior year of high school in Arkansas. Daddy was still in jail and I was motionless living with my grandparents. I love my grandparents very much but I still wanted to leave their home and live someplace else. My maternal grandmother grew to be resentful of me as she saw my father's face whenever she would look at me. I could tell she struggled with showing me kindness because her every action seemed so forced as if an invisible entity had to push her arms and legs to make her body move toward me. My granddaddy on the other hand was the reason why I was there. He was insistent upon taking care of me as if he owed me something. He cared about me because he showed me in every way he knew how. Anyway, where else was I to go? I didn't have anywhere else to go and to an extent that fact didn't matter to me. I had a restless spirit inside me and I didn't have the strength to fight with it so I gave in to it. The thought of being a burden on my grandparents plagued me everyday. My grandparents dared to call me a burden. They did not treat me that way but I felt that I was to them. So, I followed the lead of my restless spirit and started weighing my options and exploring my opportunities within my minuscule part of this huge world at the age of 16. *I'm going to make some money so I can take care of myself.* I remember telling my momma that I was going to graduate high school since my daddy did not. So I knew I had to finish high school; quitting was not an option. *What kind of job should I look for? I don't have a car so I will need to take a bus or find a job within walking distance.* I began my search for a job discreetly because I did not want anyone telling me not to find a job or discouraging my efforts in any way. I had to execute this on my own. I began to ask indirectly about various odd jobs like fast food restaurants and such. Eventually, I started earning money by ironing clothes on weekends for my track coach. I also received SSI money every month that was spent totally on bills by my grandparents. I heard my friends talking about how they chopped cotton during the summer months to make money so naturally I decided to try that, too. My grandma would drive me every morning at 5 am to the assigned bus route and pick me up at sundown. I earned $22 dollars a day chopping cotton.

Later during that month I learned that my granddaddy had lung cancer. I felt obligated to stick around to help him in any way I could—give him oxygen treatments and give him his medicines. Grandma finally told me that granddaddy had been sick for a while and they did not think it was a good idea to tell me during the time they learned of his suffering. I told granddaddy that I was still at his house because of him and that if anything ever happened to him that I was leaving his house the same day because grandma was not receptive to me at all these days. *This is death's way of toying with me by taking those I love away and keeping me alive even after my suicide attempts.* Granddaddy died later while in the hospital from complications with his cancer. We contacted family members about granddaddy's death and were able to immediately begin funeral arrangements for him. And as I told granddaddy before he died that I was leaving his house the same day he died and I did. Grandma noticed me getting my things ready to leave her house and she stated to me, "Your granddaddy told me you were going to leave when he dies." My boyfriend helped me to move in with my track team buddy—Gwen. Gwen's mother welcomed me with open arms into their home and I felt so at home with them. As I settled into my new address I started doing other chores around the house without anyone having to ask. I felt that was the least I could do because these were certainly kind people to take me in when they didn't have to. God really answered my prayer when He put me with them.

I had a boyfriend during this transition and he was respectful to them and made sure that he did not jeopardize the relationship I built with my new family. He was a really nice boy and supplied much comfort for me. And it was good that my new family liked him, too. He worked while he went to school same as I did that caused us not to spend a lot of time together but we enjoyed every minute that was spent with each other. He was my first love and best friend all wrapped up into one great person. My graduation day was two months after my granddaddy passed away. Despite all that I had experienced during my life I was so happy to see this day—graduation. I was fortunate to have my grandma, a few other relatives and my boyfriend to attend the ceremony. When my name was called to receive my diploma I felt like I was on top of the world. I could hear the faded cheers of my family and friends as I walked across the stage. At last, it was my time to feel good about something. After the ceremony ended I walked through the crowd to find my family and friends that had come see me graduate. As I walked through the crowd I heard a familiar voice calling my name, "Lisa!" I turned to see who was calling my name so desperately and to my surprise it was . . . my daddy. I almost lost my mind. *What was he doing here without my knowledge or consent? Did he really have a right just to show up unannounced? He killed my momma for God sake or did he expect me to have forgotten about her? What is wrong with this man? Furthermore, what's wrong with me, 'cause I hate my father?*

7

The Pains of Facing Fear

Dad was released from prison. I didn't visit him once while he was there. I heard he had moved into the house next door to the one he killed my momma in. He would call me and send messages to me that he wanted to see me real bad. My dad had begged me to visit him over and over again and needless to say I continued to refuse. Sure enough rumors were right because after prison he did move right next door to the house he killed my mother in. I don't know why but that was just too much for me to handle right away. Inevitably since he was now in such close range to my grandma, I ran into him at one of the corner stores one day, and was stomped with deciding whether or not to get his attention but fate made the decision for me by allow him to see me; otherwise, I might have never said anything to him. He said that I was his responsibility and no one else should have to take care of me. I wanted so badly to ask him then, *why did you take my momma from me 'cause she and you could have been taking care of me as you always did?* But I just listened to him talk as he asked over and over again for me to come and stay with him for a while. He said that I could leave if I wanted to but that I should at least give him a chance to be my daddy again. Briefly my mind drifted as he was speaking on how much my momma loved this man, my father. *She would have jumped at the opportunity to go back to him the minute she found that he was released from prison and I know that if I stay with daddy, momma would be so proud of me. Momma, why did you have to have GraveYard Love for this man?* Finally, I gave in and agreed to come to his house to stay for a while. *I agreed within myself that I would give him 1week and whether I liked it or not I'm leaving.* When I got to his house I was uncomfortable and unsure whether or not I should really be alone with him but for some reason I stayed and gave him the benefit of the doubt. I actually made it there for 3 days until he started acting strange. He never slept at night and of course I didn't either while I was there. He walked the floor more at night than during the day. I kept a weapon under my pillow just in case he decided to try . . . anything. The last night I spent there, daddy started an argument with me and I told him, "I am not my momma and I will not take your abuse!" Immediately I gathered what little I with me and left that night 'cause I didn't have graveyard love for him or nobody else. We did get another chance to talk but I never went to live at his house again.

8

A New Day

In June of 1987, at the age of 19 I was married to my first husband, Bryant Williams. I invited my daddy to be present but I did not allow him to give me away out of respect for my mother's relatives that were present and still had trouble with being in the same room with him. I asked my daddy's father to give me away but he responded, "Hell naw!" Granddaddy didn't agree with me marrying Bryant so he refused to have any part of giving me away to him. So I asked a close relative to agree to give me away and he agreed. I was expecting my first child and Bryant wanted to do the responsible thing—get married. I thought it was sweet for him not to want me to go through this experience alone so I agreed to get married. Bryant and I were planning to move to Colorado the day after our wedding because his family lived there. My daddy's parents expressed such disappointment because they had money put away from me to go to college. They had bigger dreams for me than I obviously had for myself. *I was glad to make it out of high school. I may not have been Magna Cum Laud but a thank you Laud was good enough for me.*

I still had not gotten over my momma's death or the fact that my daddy was responsible for it but I was coping the best way I knew how. So Bryant, our unborn child and I left for Colorado the very next day after our wedding. Although Bryant couldn't see it, I had more baggage with me than I could carry. Despite all that, I was happiest when I was with Bryant. We had been together since my tenth grade year of high school and his eleventh grade year. Directly after Bryant's graduation from high school he enlisted into the Army Reserve. I associated Bryant's leaving for the Army with death and longed for him very much after he left. Bryant sent me money every month while he was away which helped me greatly. I was faithful to Bryant while he was away. After being in a relationship with Bryant for 2 years Bryant asked me to marry him and to have his child. Since I needed love in any shape or form, I saw this as the perfect opportunity to build the life that I had always wanted for myself. So that was pretty much how it was for Bryant and me. Bryant and I planned our first baby; nine months later, our baby girl, Marie was born. She was the prettiest, chocolate curly haired baby I had ever seen. I was so proud to have her and loved her more than life itself. Marie resembled her granddaddy and grandma, her daddy with my smile all wrapped up into one wonderfully made little girl.

9

Unraveling

Two months before Marie was born I caught Bryant cheating on me. Although I saw him with another woman with my own eyes he tried to make me believe things were not as they seemed to be. I left Bryant and moved in with a friend from the neighborhood that was willing to let me stay with her for a while. You see Bryant and I did not have a place of our own to live yet, we were living with his sister. (As I mentioned earlier I was willing to accept anything that took on the shape or form of love even if it wasn't real.) We were living with Bryant's sister who needless to say was happy that I was leaving her brother. Bryant's sister set my belongings and everything that I had bought for my unborn baby outside on the curb after I told her that I would not keep her children while she went out to party or just because she wanted me to. Was it really fair to me for her to just leave her children with me whenever she got ready to without asking if I had anything planned to do. *Hey, I am expecting a baby in a couple of months. Doesn't she have any respect for that?* She did me a favor by putting me out of her house.

So I went to live with a neighbor and while living with the neighbor I experienced labor pains often scaring me into going to the hospital unnecessarily. Unfortunately, I would call Bryant every time I needed to go to the hospital, which he complained about because he had to leave work often. On the evening that Marie was born Bryant took me to the hospital and complained the whole ride there about how much time he was wasting on taking me to the hospital just to have me sent back home without a baby. Well, Marie finally came and she and I took a bus back to Arkansas the next day.

I had contacted my daddy's momma and told her what was happening in my life and she welcomed me back with opened arms and without judgment. I had very little money so my baby had to drink regular Vitamin D milk because I couldn't prepare the formula on our very tiring and extensive road trip back to Arkansas. I managed to survive the trip with a new baby and all of my post-partum issues. Looking back in retrospect, I was willing to withstand as much physical pain that could be inflicted on me but I *did not* want to hurt anymore in my brain. I delighted in the idea of just taking a deep breath without wondering about Bryant. I was so happy to see my family when I got to Arkansas but even more happy to get Marie and me off that bus. I headed straight for grandma's house where I knew I could get comfortable and someone else to hold Marie for a while. However, when I got there I could not get comfortable enough to just settle in something inside my spirit just kept tugging on me. It was called The Bond of Marriage. I had been in Arkansas for only 4 days when Bryant showed up after driving all the way from Colorado to get Marie and me. I guessed Bryant had realized his mistakes and decided that he wanted his family more than another woman. I could not resist Bryant so I returned to Colorado with him and we moved in with his brother. After returning to Colorado it wasn't long before feelings of regret slapped me right in the face. My marriage to Bryant began to suffer worse than ever before. He started again staying out all night long. I would go out looking for him most of the time and even called the police and hospitals making inquiries on several occasions. I was just so dumb and naïve to what could actually be in the heart and mind of not only another human being but to one who professed to love me. Well, before I could leave him again Bryant claimed to have a solution to our problems. Bryant decided we should get our own place to stay and that our marriage would get better soon afterwards, "You'll see," said Bryant. Since we had never had a place of our own I couldn't express how happy I was to hear that soon we would have more room and privacy in our own space. *Things have to get better when we move.* I was completely convinced things would get better and that we had found *it*—our solution.

10

Bits and Pieces

Finally, our very own place to live—no in-laws or relatives it was just Bryant, the baby and me. The apartment was everything I hoped it would be. The apartment complex was a really nice one, too. The neighborhood was quiet and the building was secured as a gated community. Yeah, everything was proper. My husband's job wasn't far from home so everything seemed perfect. I got a job at the post office and was able to find a trustworthy church going lady to watch over our little angel.

Our marriage seemed to be getting better, too. Our jobs were holding up well and baby Marie was healthy—all was well. My heart was elated and finally at peace until . . . the night Bryant didn't come home. Since we were in an apartment of our own I found myself staying with him and allowing him to beat me down emotionally as I dealt with his infidelity. I found myself crying night after night wondering what I had done wrong, how could I make him love me the way he used to. He used to make me feel valuable but all of a sudden I'm sitting outside on garbage day awaiting my one last chance to be someone's treasure. *I knew it wasn't the baby that drove him away 'cause he would always show Marie so much love plus on top of that Marie was planned. So why was he doing this? Why was he kicking us to the curb? Why weren't the baby and I enough for him? What am I supposed to do now? Then the answer came to me ... momma stayed with daddy while he was cheating on her so maybe she was teaching me to do the same thing. I'm supposed to stay here with my husband while he sleeps around. This is my lot in life, huh? Am I supposed to continue to let him make love to me, too? Momma, why did you have to love daddy so much maybe even more than me? I need you now more than ever? I need someone to hold Marie just long enough for me to go to the bathroom. I know you would be able to help me if you were here. God, help me through this pain. My spirit is in bits and pieces right now and I need you to put me back together again, right now!! I don't know how much more I can take before I loose my mind.*

Several months passed and my self-esteem continued to drag the ground digging trenches along my tiresome journey just to make it from day to day. I hated to wake up in the mornings. Marie's bright smile turned in to torrid screams because I was no longer any use to her either. I became physically ill and in constant abdominal pain so I decided to see a doctor. The doctors treated me for an infection and depression. Meanwhile, as I waited to be called upon at the doctor's office a lady not many years older than myself by the name of Patina struck up a conversation with me. She asked what church I belonged to but it wasn't until then that I realized that I had not been to church since I had lived in Colorado.

11

Weeping May Endure for a Night . . . But Joy's Coming In the Morning

Patina and I became very good friends and as a matter of fact, I believed that God sent me an angel in the form of a friend. I made her my baby girl's godmother because she helped to take such good care of her. I was going through so much at home and keeping so much locked inside until I literally could not catch my breath at times. Patina would stay on the phone with me for hours talking to me and lifting my spirits; besides, my husband wasn't home more than he was home.

I finally got enough courage to leave Bryant again but I was still in an emotional wreck. It was tough but I stayed with Patina, **my friend**. I'd finally found someone on **my** side for a change. Patina would allow Bryant over to visit Marie but only if she could tell I was emotionally having a good day. Patina would pray with me because most times I did not feel like praying since my spirit had become so beat down. Patina showed me exactly what I believe what my momma would have wanted me to see in myself—that I desperately needed Jesus. After staying with Patina for a while I started visiting her church with her and soon felt spiritually stronger. I was even able to talk to Bryant about the church services when he would visit Marie and me. I felt renewed when I started going back to church. I felt so good until I went back with Bryant to live in our apartment again. This time Bryant didn't wait twenty-four hours to start staying out all night again—he didn't come in when he dropped Marie and me off at the apartment. He immediately started hanging out with his brothers and friends. He would come home and I would find phone numbers, pictures of women and sometimes pictures of them with their children. (The children weren't his to my knowledge.) I was so fed up with finding *player paraphernalia.* At first I was looking for concrete signs of his cheating ways but after a while the signs found me. One particular night when Bryant didn't come home at all, I got brave enough to call the most recent telephone number I had found in one of his pockets. When she answered the phone I thought I would start in on her with all kinds of profanity and name-calling but I didn't. I asked, "Is Bryant there?" She answered, "No." "Who is this?" I answered, "*His wife.*" *Sheila* was her name.

12

Unbelievable

I know I told you, reader, at the beginning of this book when I was born so I didn't just fall off a turnip truck yesterday, so what makes this husband of mine think it's alright for his hoes to call this house? Yeah, that's right, now the girlfriends and I are calling each other looking for Bryant.

By now, when Bryant doesn't come home yes it hurts, but I have run out of suggestions on what I should do about it. When he came home one particular morning, he came in looking like a scared cat in the middle of a dog patch. "I been in jail," he said. I just looked at him without even asking why. He sat on the couch for a while in deep thought. I called his name several times; he never answered. *I hope he is thinking about what a mess he is making of his life.* He stood up suddenly and walked to the phone directory, picked it up and picked up the phone. I asked who he was about to call and he replied "Patina's pastor." *Why is it that when a person goes to jail they also pick up religion too? Do the jails have infinite amounts of religion in stock and keep it where the inmates can get as much as they want on the way in? Well, come to think of it, I had been in jail too—in my mind and wouldn't you know that I ended up at church myself.* I was happy to hear him mention anybody's pastor at this point. When he got the pastor on the phone; of course, he asked Bryant when he was planning to make a visit to the church? I knew Pastor had asked him because Bryant's response was, "I'll be there Sunday." We rose that Sunday morning after preparing our clothes the Saturday night before. I got little Marie fed, dressed and ready to go while Bryant waited on us. Not long after arriving at the church, Pastor made acknowledgements of the visitors. Reader, in case you have never been to an African American church with fewer than one hundred members to show up at one time, you'll find it easy to spot guest from regular members from where the Pastor sits. Bryant stood up and I stood with Marie by his side as his support I was so proud once again to be Mrs. Lisa Williams. For just a few minutes I felt wonderful about our future together. My husband introduced himself to the church and told everyone that he had been a member of another church where he was a Sunday school teacher. He then stated that he would like to place his name along with his families' as a member of this church. I immediately started dancing and shouting praises to God for answering my prayers.

Bryant knew all the right moves to make and all the right things to say in order to slowly gain my trust again while sliding into his old slippery, slimy snake-like ways.

After his willingness to show up to church to make everybody believe that he was so sincere about attending regularly, he didn't show up again for another 2-3 months.

13

Healing My Way

I continued to attend church regularly—the baby and me. Eventually the church members stopped asking about my husband and started saying, "Tell Brother Bryant I said hey and that I miss seeing him here." I admit I had been nagging Bryant about going to church until I noticed that wasn't keeping him from getting up and dressed to go someplace else on Sunday mornings. God gave me inner peace as I watched Bryant do what he wanted to do and that rarely included anything with Marie or me. I found myself reciting the *Serenity Prayer* often as a reminder that I do not control others only myself.

One Sunday morning I kept silent as I repeated the *Serenity Prayer* over and over in my head as Bryant asked me, "Why you not fussing this morning 'cause you know I'm not going to church this morning?" I was so into repeating the prayer in my head I didn't hear him at first but then I replied, "Huh?" He repeated, "Why you not fussing 'cause you know I'm not going to church with you?" I recognized the evil forces that were driving my husband to reject me—they were the same evil forces that rejected God's power and authority and caused Jesus to be nailed to the cross. I calmly stated to Bryant, "Bryant, I'm not fussing about that anymore." Bryant left the house before I did and I didn't see him until two o'clock the next morning. I had trouble sleeping later that night and decided to sit on the steps outside the apartments. All of a sudden I saw a huge tow truck with what looked like my husband's car being pulled on the back of it. As the tow truck got closer to the security gates I could see it better and it *was* my husband's car being towed and my husband was riding shotgun in the tow truck. Bryant didn't look a bit surprised to see me sitting outside at two in the morning as he walked past me and said, "I don't know why I don't listen to you." Bryant had been in a horrible accident earlier that night. His car flipped over several times but he walked away without a scratch on him. He was blessed to have walked away from the accident alive and without being hurt at all. When I got back inside the apartment he just broke down in tears and instantly I thought of all the horrible things I could have said to him but I did not say them; instead, I walked over to him and just hugged him to show him that I love him and want him to understand that I only want what is best for us as a family and for him to accept that God dispatched angels to protect him tonight night and I am glad He did.

14

Victim or Criminal

I survived many of my husband's secret lovers during my marriage to him and even had one over for dinner. We actually enjoyed each other's company as we had many conversations together. However, she told me some very hurtful things about my husband. For starters she told me that he told her that he wasn't married and that he was getting custody of our daughter because I . . . (he tells her) I was on drugs. This woman did have the decency to tell me that she would not have been with him had she known he was married. *But the woman is still here now that she knows he is married so I guess it's good of me to find the good in this situation, huh?*

Let's back up for just a minute . . . When Bryant learned that his lover was coming over to our house he lost all his cool points. He started yelling and screaming, "That b . . . ain't coming in this house!! I replied, "Oh, yes she is, too." He says, "Well, I'm leaving then." She arrived an hour after Bryant had already left. She and I were very cordial with each other—she was extremely complimentary toward my daughter and me. She stated how she couldn't understand why he would be out cheating on his wife and neglecting his baby like that. She also asked, "How can you look *me* in the eyes knowing I have been sleeping with 'yo husband?" I couldn't help but to tell her that God let me know what was happening before now, so I've had some time to deal with the issue outside of her presence. Thanks be to God for his mercy and grace in that instance (or maybe she should be saying that). *Remember reader, if you don't want to know the truth about something then don't ask God about because HE can't lie, but if you want to know be ready to accept the truth however it comes, especially if you ask God to tell you anyway. God deals with us to make us strong and for us to give Him glory—I want Him to get his glory, too. I was living a saved and separated life for God as much as I knew how while I was continually hurt emotionally spiritually by the man that I had once loved more than life itself. You see reader, the enemy, which is the devil, made me believe that I couldn't make it on my own so I was co-dependent on Bryant until one day I had had enough.

Bryant told me that he was moving out of the apartment. The next day Bryant was still there so I told him that I would leave since he was still there. I found my cousin's ex-husband and stayed with him for a while since he was like family to me. After several days of that I moved in with a female co-worker of mine. I felt sorry for myself, lonely and depressed more often now than not. So I decided to return to the carnal ways of living and dealing with hurt and pain—sex, drugs and alcohol.

15

From The Skillet to the Frying Pan

My body could take only so much loneliness so I started dating a young man from work, who we will refer to as Cato. Time wasn't long before we moved in together. I was still legally married to Bryant although we had been separated for quite some time. Cato and I had lived together for a year when I learned that I was pregnant with my second child. I admit I was in a s-e-v-e-r-e state of confusion. I did manage to file for a divorce, which was finalized the day after my son was born and yes I showed up in court that same day. The judge asked if the child that I had just given birth to was husband Bryant's and of course my reply was, "No." The judge declared us legally divorced at that time. Cato and I considered marriage but I was hesitant because he had to have his 40oz. of beer everyday if possible. Just like my dad did with momma, Cato worked and gave me the check to pay bills with while he smoked and drank his problems away. So far things were well between us and I had found peace in church again shortly after meeting Cato.

One night while I went to church, Cato was home with our son who I named Karl. When I got to church I could not get into the worship service like I wanted to and I kept feeling a pulling inside to leave there and return home immediately. After several minutes of that tugging I left before the service was over. It was as though God was making me leave the church service that night. *But why would God do that?* When I got home I saw Cato passed out on the floor and our son face down on a blood soaked couch lying still as a log. *"God please no, not my baby. Don't take my baby."* I slowly turned over our son and saw faint movement of his chest but just above his eye was a gash in his skin that had split wide open. I wanted to know what happened so I tried to remain calm while I tried to wake Cato from his drunken stupor to ask him what happened. Of course, that whole scenario even today makes my emotions flare. I found myself wanting to snatch Cato's soul from his body but I kept a level head so that I could help my baby. I struggled to remember remedies that my momma and grandma would use on me when I was a young child. I was able to recall a time when I fell on some iron and split my wrist open. I jumped up and grabbed bandages, alcohol, peroxide, ointments, gauze and towels. I prayed to God while I worked on my son at home. Meanwhile Cato still lay passed out on the floor as he slowly came to himself in intervals. Cato wanted to take the baby to the hospital but I explained to him that if we take him to the hospital under these circumstances in which he got hurt: "You were drunk and I was gone which equals neglect and the state officials coming to take my baby." *I was not about to let that happen.* So I didn't have to worry about anybody else taking my baby because after that incident I took my own baby and left Cato in the trailer house that *I* was buying. I had the deed to the trailer transferred over to him and made all other necessary arrangements for him to live there. I suggested that he find a reliable roommate so he wouldn't have to go back to his parents' house. I understand now when his mom told me that he always ends up back at their house when his relationships don't work out. So I was alone once again and went right back to the sex and alcohol. I went to clubs with my friends from work so that I could dance. I could rock the house with my dances. Everybody wanted to drink and meet other people but I wanted to dance and talk to people in the club about the Lord. I talked to a young man one time and he told me to be quiet because he was going to "shoot up the place." God spared my life and others that night. That guy carried out his plan and didn't miss his target either. Although I went to the club, I still loved the Lord but I was acting out signs of rebellion because of my deep hurts and pains inside. I started behaving like a sinner more and more because I was able to get my mind off the things I had been through. I continued to go out with my friends as if my conscience had been seared with an iron.

My children stayed with their grandparents and great-grandparents when I went out with friends and during the summers they lived with them. The cycle spun again and landed on me meeting another young man who seemed really kind, Devin. He was an organist in church and boy could he sing like a bird. We talked all the time and he finally asked me out. He expressed to me what kind of woman he was looking for and the type of relationship he desired to have with her and wouldn't you know that his descriptions sounded a lot like me. Now, he was not the best looking man but he dressed nicely and talked a real smooth game for a church boy. He knew exactly what I wanted to hear. He wined and dined me weekly. After several months of dating we had spent most of our time in church together. I went to church with him often because he was the Minister of Music there and couldn't be absent like I could from my church without a penalty.

Summer was over and the children were coming back home to Colorado. Since Devin was from Helena, Arkansas he volunteered to drive me to Brentwood to pick up my children. I stayed there with my grandma and he went to stay with his mother at her house while he was visiting in Arkansas. As I said earlier the cycle spun and spun then stopped on . . . *living together*. Yes, Devin and I made the decision to live together. This time it only took about six months for the monster in the man to manifest. He started disrespecting me by talking to other women in my presence. He would pick up women and take them to work with me in the car and take their phone calls at home with me sitting right there. But at the same time he would show up on my job and question me about who I was talking to. I told him, "You know I work in the men's department at this store so I have to talk to men and the conversation is about merchandise not me." He was like a chameleon because I did not see that he was green with envy and black with evil when I met him. He started acting very possessive and started working on tearing down my self-esteem by saying things like, "You ain't nothing." and "Don't nobody want you." Things had gotten so bad until we started arguing about anything. He would hit me and of course, I started fighting him back. Once he got so mad he started hitting me then grabbed me and threw me down. I told him that I wouldn't stand for his behavior. He would apologize then later start up all over again. I was living in a facility where I was not supposed to have a man inside the house with me but the landlord tolerated it from me as long as she could borrow my money. But one day I got an eviction notice giving me twenty-four hours to get out. Sure enough Devin had been staying there when he should not have been but I guess we had one too many fights. An anonymous tenant turned me in to the landlord. I had to get out although I had nowhere else to go. My children were allowed to stay with Cato's sister (my son's aunt) and I slept in my car for the next two months.

 Cato got an apartment and I moved in with him until I could find a place of my own to stay. As usual we fought so much until I just got physically tired. One Sunday before church we had been fighting in the car and I started to remember some things from my past and got the biggest adrenaline rush to claw his face and neck until I drew blood and it dripped all over his lily white shirt that *I* ironed for him to wear. My Pastor at that time knew that we had a violent relationship and had suggested that we separate before someone gets hurt, goes to jail or dies. When I would try to leave Devin, things would always get calm again but the calm was because the storm was coming. The ugly demons of abuse would unfailingly show up—verbal, psychological, emotional and physical. He even stooped so low as to say he always wanted a light-skinned woman with long hair. I asked him, "Why you with me then?" I thought about it for a few seconds and came up with the answer myself—*why wouldn't he take everything he could get from me for free if I allowed him to.* He was getting all the privileges of a husband without having to be one or assume the responsibility of one. And out of all I gave him, Devin kept up his rituals of telling me that I was nothing and that I would never to be nothing.

We had been fighting one night in particular in front of the children and my son broke out into tears. A light bulb finally went off in my head. We left there at one o'clock in the morning walking. We made it to my friend's house around the corner. Devin knew exactly where I would go when we would have fights and sure enough he showed up there making a scene. And since I didn't want to jeopardize the good thing my friend had going for her I got my children and left with Devin. And what a huge mistake because I only returned to the same crap that took me so long to work up the nerve to leave. Now, I would have to wait on my next opportunity to feel strong enough to leave again for hopefully for good.

16

Can't Win For Losing

Devin and I argued endlessly so it seemed. I finally got the nerve to involve the police to make him leave the apartment 'cause me leaving him wasn't working. When the police arrived I told them that I wanted Devin out of the apartment because my name was on the lease and not his name. Well, to my surprise Devin was able to produce a lease agreement with both his signature and mine. *Where did he? . . . How did he . . . No this nigga didn't go behind my back and put his name on my lease without telling me. I can't win for losing with him in my life. God, how can I get rid of him?* "Devin you are a snake!" "Devin, you are the devil" I yelled. The police said, "Ma'am he has just as much right to stay here as you do and by law I cannot make him leave without a lawful reason." And since things had not been physical this time ole Devin was standing there looking like a saint and getting so much pleasure out of watching my defeat in front of the police. I was utterly disgusted.

I spent so many nights crying it almost got to the point I needed to cry to fall asleep. Sometimes during the day Devin would come home during his lunch break thinking that he would catch me with another man. *As a man thinks so he is—that's what the Bible says.* But little did he know I was preoccupied with how to **get away** from a man not be with one. Once Devin would come inside the apartment and see that I had not been with anyone else inside, and then he would try to get me to have sex with him. I always refused because there was nothing internal to make me desire him anymore. Obviously, it wasn't about desire for him because he would not accept no for an answer and he would force me to have sex with him. Yes, he raped me after everything he had already done to me. I was convinced that he did not care anything about me the way he just took sex from me. I felt so trapped because I had nowhere else to go and no money to get there. Besides Devin seemed to find me wherever I went.

I caught the bus to work when Devin wouldn't take me. He mostly agreed to take me to work when I was scheduled on the evening shift. Through it all I admit I did some stupid things like giving him the money to pay the rent but instead he left me and didn't pay the rent. That was all the money I had until my next paycheck for two weeks. He moved out taking everything he had and all that I could give. I was so angry with him! Well, I was mad because *he* left *me*. Fortunately, I still had three days to get my rent paid, but where was I going to get the money? I called relatives—they were unable to help. I called my pastor—he had a death in the family and was unable to get through to him. I called church members and they felt a need to ask the pastor's permission to loan me money to keep a roof over my head. No one could help me. I didn't understand why the church that I pay tithes to could not help me when I needed it most.

I was frantic so I started thinking on how I could get my children to my grandma so they wouldn't have to be on the street with me. I was starting to feel hopeless so I prayed and reminded God that I have been trusting Him the best ways I knew how and now all I have is my faith. Now, faith without works is dead. Right now, I am working to stay strong considering my circumstances. I had only one day left to pay my rent and I still did not have any more resources to go to. So the children and I decided to go outside and while we were out I stopped to get the mail from our box and wouldn't you know that I had not one but two child support checks from Bryant that added up to just a little more than what was needed to cover my rent. God will work miracles for the just as well as the unjust. I was not worthy of God's grace and mercy but He is quick to give it and liberal with His love.

Three weeks later Devin was back in the apartment and what a horrible mistake that was. My self-esteem was at an all time low. I didn't want to go to work because I didn't want to go outside the apartment. I continued to feel dependent upon him because he had a car and I didn't. I thought I needed him to help me take the children to the daycare center and school. Needless to say I was not the only one getting worse off mentally because Devin started following me to work and spying on me there. He would hide behind shelves going from isle to isle in the department store watching me and trying his best to catch me doing something he felt I shouldn't have been doing. I was so uncomfortable during this time in my life. If he thought I was looking at a man, Devin would ask, "Do you know that nigga?" My response was always that I'm not looking at anyone particular, but no matter what, he never believed me. So there I was continuing to live in misery.

17

Help Is On the Way

By now you know, Reader, I have plenty of relatives especially cousins. Well, I had a cousin to call me that I hadn't heard from in quite some time and unfortunately she was calling with bad news—her baby had been born dead, stillborn. She called to inform me of the funeral and to express how much she would appreciate me being there with her if at all possible. Certainly was my first reaction and shock and empathy the next. That call brought back to my mind every ounce of tragedy I had been through in my lifetime. Immediately I could see my momma's face of approval at my positive response to my cousin's news. I sat there a moment until my momma's face faded once again from my sight. I was given a chance to focus on someone else's misfortune rather than my own. I had to tell Devin the news about my cousin's baby because I wanted him to take me to the funeral. His response was as heartless as all the rest of his actions toward me as he quickly stated, "Why she having a funeral? It ain't like she knew it. You can use the car 'cause I ain't going."

I woke up the next morning and got my daughter ready for school and my son ready for daycare as I always did. Devin was gone as usual and I was supposed to have gotten another way to work and he left me the car but to my surprise when I walked out the front door to leave there was no car to be found in the parking lot. I was infuriated. With no time to waste I started walking the children to school. As I headed back home what did I see but Devin's car at the traffic light but he was not driving someone else was and beside his car was Devin's sister's car with Devin driving it. I could tell he didn't want me to notice him as he sped off when the traffic light changed to green. The cars quickly drove out of view as they went separate ways but minutes later Devin's car pulled up beside me as I walked toward home. Meanwhile the car stopped with one of his friends behind the wheel. "What's up, I'm Robert," he said. "I know who you are but you don't know me. Devin said for me to bring you the car after I got finished using it." I was totally pissed but got behind the wheel of the car that Devin's friend had so conveniently used asked if I needed to take *him* anywhere, waited on his answer, he replied, "Naw, I'm straight," I wanted to know what was really going on but I knew Devin was up to his ole paranoia infused ways so I refused to stoop to his way of thinking and decided to focus on my own plans for that day. I made it to the apartment and got dressed for the funeral.

On my way to my cousin's house before the funeral I noticed Devin's sister's car with him still behind the wheel following me pathetically as he tried to be inconspicuously slick-like. Just to be sure it was him I made a few fancy maneuvers of my own and sure enough he followed suit. "Idiot!!" I screamed. As I parked the car in my cousin's apartment complex I continued to act like I didn't see him pull into the parking lot seconds later after I did. I got out of the car and headed to my cousin's apartment door so that we could ride together to the funeral. My cousin greeted me with open arms and a tearful face. As much as I hated to I proceeded to tell her about the foolish man I had become involved with that was now in the parking lot spying on me instead of being at work. While my cousin continued to get ready for the funeral I left to fill the tank with gas and of course, the idiot followed. I pulled into the gas station and jumped out the car and stood looking directly at him. Our eyes finally met then I asked him if he was tired of following me yet? *Why is he following me? Why is he so possessive or should I say possessed? I have never cheated on him with anyone so what was his problem?* When I got back to my cousin's apartment several of my other relatives had arrived and met me in the parking lot only to find that they were waiting on Devin. They surrounded Devin's car when he pulled up. They said if he ever thought of putting his hands on me again that he would answer to them. Inside I felt so much vindication from them protecting me like that. Devin's only reply was, "I hear you, mane." I looked at him and told him that it was over and that I'd have his car back to him later. I never moved back in with him from that day to this one.

18

Joy Comes From Within

Today is a new day. I am living with a girlfriend of mine who encouraged me to apply for section eight housing 'til I can do better financially. I prayed so hard 'cause the waiting list was incredibly long. I was willing to wait though, 'cause right now I should live alone—with just my children and me. I was told that I could be waiting for years before I hear a reply from the housing authority. I believe that when man says no God can still say yes . . . and He did. I got a call three weeks later notifying me of a vacancy. I was able to see the house the same day of the call and loved it. Life was finally turning out good. I worked only four blocks from home at a hospital as a Certified Nursing Assistant and Transporter. I was even the first African American to work in the hospital's Recovery Unit (so I was told). I noticed other African Americans being hired after I'd been working for a while. I worked there two years and could not have been happier with my children and my life.

I'd made a really good friend who we will refer to as Yogi. She too was a Godsend. She took care of my children while I worked two jobs. I still went out on the town every once in a while just to relieve some stress and it worked well for me for a while. One night while my friends and I were out at a club, I noticed a young man wearing a hood who I had never seen before (most of us were regulars and not wearing hoods). He looked like he was up to something no good. I got a feeling that was overwhelming inside of me so I alerted my friends and they agreed to leave with me. After getting home I received a phone call around one in the morning from a cousin of mine asking if I had gone to the club that night. I let her know that I was there with some of friends but we left around eleven o'clock that night. She proceeded to tell me about a shooting that happened around midnight with four people pronounced dead at the scene. It was then that I started paying more attention to the voice of the Lord and how He would deal with me inwardly to give me warnings. It was definitely God that kept us that night from being in the wrong place at the wrong time. After that incident, I didn't want to take the voice of God for granted at all and was so grateful that I listened that time. That was my last taste of the club's nightlife.

I attended the funerals of those young men that died at the club that night and watched as their gang brothers gathered together and wore their colors, as a sign that payback was coming for the deaths of their "gang" brothers. The sight of those uniformed colors standing around the wall of that funeral home will never leave my mind. I could relate to the feelings of wanting to pay an eye for an eye, but I refused to allow those feelings to overtake me because vengeance does not belong to me but to GOD. This scenario only made me appreciate God's grace and mercy; especially since I am not deserving of it. I spent more time praying for other people more than ever because when I take my mind off my own situation God can take care of me completely without me getting in His way. I started realizing that some people were unaware of God's presence and He keeps us from the 'wiles of the devil' everyday and has and our peace and safety have nothing to do with anything that we do or are capable of doing because good people die too. My momma died and I thought of her as a living saint. Moreover, Jesus died and He did no wrong.

    The shootings of those young men brought back the pain for me of my momma's death. I realized I had not healed from it yet. I just couldn't get the sound of gunshots out of my head. It seemed to be all types of guns—big and small sounding off in my head like the Fourth of July. Many nights I had nightmares. I spent countless days in states of deep depression. I recall telling my roommate how thankful I was to God for protecting me even when I was indulged in my carnal ways trying to find relief and not thinking of Him, but only thinking of a way to make my body feel relief from the stresses of life by dancing and drinking. *What did drinking and dancing in the club that have to do with telling someone how good God is? Did my going to the club convince anyone to accept Jesus as their Savior? Besides, drawing people to Christ is what I was put here to do.* So I continued to pray for others and I found a new release of positive energy in forgetting about my own suffering. I prayed that those gang members would have a change of heart and decide not to take matters into their own hands. Since those young men are so filled with rage and anger they got revenge on those responsible for killing their gang brothers. *But was killing going to make anybody come back from the dead?* So, I continued to pray for those young men and others that were in unbearable pain.

19

The Prayer Line

After the club shootings I spent every chance I got in church. I finally became an active member. I even joined the Usher Board. My friend Yogi and I went to church one Sunday night and to our surprise the pastor had an aluminum tub filled with 'blessed oil.' (Reader, in case you are not familiar with the term-blessed oil, this is virgin olive oil poured into tiny vials to be dispensed to each member. The oil is sometimes left on the alter of the church for several days at which time prayers are said to God to put His anointing into every drop of the oil that will be given to his people to use as they need.)

This particular night the pastor instructed us to take off our shoes and to line up and walk through the oil. Now, I admit at first I was acting like the children of Israel when they questioned Moses about where they were going before they reached Canaan, but I snapped out of it 'cause I didn't want to end up like some of them that never crossed over to the Promised Land. So I looked at Yogi and said, "Well girl, we have served on this Usher Board together and even partied in the clubs together so I don't know about you but I'm giving my life back to God 'cause I need Him—His guidance. God has been too good to me even when I wasn't focusing on making Him. She looked at me with tears in her eyes and replied, "Me too." We both got in line and walked through the oil 'til we reached pastor at the end of the line. All I could see was my pastor standing there waiting with his hand dripping with olive oil waiting to lay hands on my forehead. When the pastor laid his hand on my head something happened to me and I blacked out completely. All I remember is waking up on the other side of the sanctuary feeling light as a feather. It was as though all of my worries and problems had been lifted from my shoulders. I knew this feeling was a visit from God's Holy Spirit.

My friend, Yogi and I started visiting other churches when we could. I remember when we had trouble finding this one particular church but we were determined to find it 'cause we knew that when we were able to find it blessing waiting on us. Yogi and I finally stopped at the neighborhood store and asked for help to the church and wouldn't you know there was a lady inside able to take us directly to it. When we got inside the building it was packed with people like mackerels in a can. Not long after the usher found Yogi and I a couple of seats, this elderly mother in the church jumped up and began to speak in tongues. [Now, reader allow me to explain to those of you unfamiliar with the gift of speaking in unknown tongues before you decide to judge this poe 'lil ole lady who is worshipping God according to her understanding. We believe that unknown tongues come directly from the Holy Spirit. It is the Spirit's way of communicating to God what we are unable to speak of naturally and when spoken in public the tongues are usually followed by an interpreter so that the entire body of people will understand what has been said or asked of the people.] Now with all that said, allow me to continue with the 'lil ole lady speaking in tongues. She also interpreted what had been said: "The Lord has spoken and said destruction is upon a young man among us here tonight." The Pastor then stood and confirmed what the mother had spoken to be true when he replied, "I had a conversation with another Minister earlier today and he told me that he felt death hovering over the young people of our town." Young people were everywhere in this building tonight. The pastor asked all the young people to stand and hold hands as the Elders prayed a special prayer of protection for each young person there that night. After that prayer, the Pastor asked that all the young men in the church would line up for individual prayer. Most of the young men complied and stood patiently in line; except for one young man whose eyes were blood shot red and his voice so deep like he spoke from the pits hell. When the Pastor got to him he asked the young man, "May I pray for you young man?" The young man's voice replied, "No!" This surprised the entire congregation except for the Pastor, I think. He looked as though he expected the boy to reject prayer. All the ministers inside the sanctuary started walking toward the boy and Pastor as if to surround the two of them. One of the ministers gave Pastor a vial of blessed oil that he drenched his hands in. The boy fell to the ground and began to slither underneath the church pews before Pastor was able to touch him with his oil-drenched hands. That's right I said slither. Several Ministers were able to restrain the boy and got him to the center of the sanctuary but were unable to stand him up on the floor. So the ministers continued to restrain the boy and began putting oil on his head and into his mouth as they prayed and commanded the evil spirits within the boy to release him. This went on for several minutes until the boy showed signs of compliance.

Suddenly the boy began to speak out with praises to God for delivering him; he even quoted a scripture. The boy really did look different to me now—his eyes were white again instead of red and his countenance looked brighter and not hazy as it did at first. The boy stated, "I am free. I will never be the same." The entire congregation went up in a roar of praise to God for delivering the boy from the demons that wanted to kill him. I had always heard about these types of instances happening in Pentecostal churches but I had never seen it for myself until this night. I am convinced that demons are real. I had arrived at yet another reason for getting closer to God. This experience gave me a new outlook on my expectations from God—He will be to us exactly what we allow him to be. Although I was still dealing with many of my issues of life, I believed that God would deliver me from all of them.

20

Taking My Life Back

"It's time for you to go back home." I began to look around until I heard it again. "It's time for you to go back home." I knew then that God was telling me to go back to Arkansas. "Why?" I asked God, when I have everything here that I need—I have a good job, section eight housing, and my grandparents in my life and you Lord that's all I need. After three months of struggling with whether or not to listen to the voice of God, I told God, "Okay, I'll go back." I know if you are telling me to go back then you will put everything in order for me to make it happen. When Sunday came I was able to tell my church family that I was leaving for Arkansas. They were not happy about the news but they wanted me to obey God. Some of them even helped me to sell some of my belongings from my apartment that I didn't want to take with me. I gave away many things like clothes and shoes and some furniture. I sold my car to a neighbor. My best friend Yogi left with me for Arkansas stayed there for two weeks then left for Mexico.

When I arrived in Arkansas, I was able to live with my daddy and grandma. My children were used to being here during the summer months and were very much settled in. My daddy and I talked briefly discussing the living arrangements and my desire for him to deal only with the children when he is sober. My children love him so much I just couldn't keep them from him, but I had to set boundaries. My new job came quite easily although I wasn't making the amount of money I desired; I stayed with it for the next several weeks regardless. I told God I wanted a job making more money because I needed to help out my daddy and grandma plus I have two children to take care of as a single parent. My grandmother told me of a job prospect. I checked it out and later went for a weight test since it consisted of lifting packages. While I waited my turn with others at the office we were all graced with the presence of a very outspoken young man that seemed to know no strangers. While the group waited to be called on by the interviewing staff this young man talked and talked. I guess he was uncomfortable with silence. After the long wait at the first appointment I was given yet another appointment scheduled for one week to fill out paperwork for the company's records.

So one week later I showed up to complete my paperwork, as I was eager to start the paychecks rolling in. As I was writing I looked up and who but Mr. Talk-A-Lot from last week shows up. I try really hard not to make eye contact with him 'cause I was not giving him a reason to start his motor running. But wouldn't you know Talk-A-Lot had a good memory, too, when I looked up he immediately recognized me from last week which he made seem like yesterday. When he sat next to me and started talking I asked him, "Do you love God more than you love yourself?" He said, "Yes, I do." I noticed then how well dressed he was and how actually pleasant he was.

After turning in all the paperwork, I was asked to prepare myself for a mandatory drug test that was to occur immediately. I was more than ready so I thought. I realized I needed to drink some water to make some because I didn't feel the need to give a sample. Since it took me several minutes to drink enough water, Mr. You Know Who walked by preparing himself for his drug test, too. He was still waving like we were seeing each other for the first time today. While I sat down to wait on my urge to go in a cup, Mr. Talk-A-Lot came and sat next to me. He asked how I was doing and I replied, "not good." "What's wrong?" he asked. "I can't seem to give them enough urine so just pray for me so I can." Reader, can you believe he put his hands together and started praying right there in the waiting room? And the real showstopper—when prayer was over I had to go immediately—to pee. After filling up my cup the toilet overflowed. I left the restroom after having more water now than I know what to do with. Mr. Talk-A-Lot was standing right at the door when I walked out. "How did everything come out?" he asked. "Unstoppable. It was like witnessing a miracle" I replied. He looked at me and said, "My name is Terrance." We shook hands, "I'm Lisa," I said. "Lisa, can I call you sometime?" "No, I'm staying with my grandma and I won't disrespect her home, but I can call you if you want me to." "Sure, thing" he said. I waited on my ride home with continual thoughts of the miracle that had just taken place in the restroom. When I got my first paycheck, I was able to pay my daddy's parole officer once a month and made sure he kept his appointments with her as scheduled. I gave daddy his cigarette money weekly and bought him clothes when he needed them. When daddy needed to go to the unemployment office I took him to fill out his paperwork. It wasn't 'til then that I learned my daddy could not read and could only write his name. I also realized then that *I love my father very much despite fact he murdered my momma.*

21

Letting Go and Letting God

I received the news that my maternal grandma was in the hospital. I immediately found my way to her hospital room. When I saw her I asked her to forgive me for anything I may have done to her that I shouldn't have. You see grandma harbored plenty of bitterness toward my daddy for killing her baby girl, Martha, and the fact that I looked just like daddy didn't help her matters much either. I did everything I could to please grandma but it seemed nothing I did was ever good enough for her. But grandpa, momma's daddy, on the other hand, he was my bosom buddy, which is why when grandpa died I got outta dodge. Well, as I was saying grandma was now on her sick bed and as I asked her to forgive me for all that I had done wrong I also let her know that I may not be sick today but tomorrow is not promised to me either.

After that visit with grandma in the hospital, I thought I might pay a visit to some other relatives that I had deep issues with. I visited with them and asked them to forgive me for our misunderstandings and everyone parted peacefully. I lost four family members within that year and was still feeling the pain of losing them all. I knew that God had given me the desire to apologize to each of my relatives so that I could start letting go and letting God do what He had planned for me in the first place—which is to please Him. Daddy and I have become closer than we've ever been before because directly following momma's death I could not stand to be in the same room with him without feeling like running away or like I would lose my mind if I had to listen to him apologize one more time. I still have a hard time with the memories of surrounding momma's death when I don't have work, children or other people to focus on but I'm forced by the power of life to carry on with my life. *How long exactly am I allowed to be mad at my daddy—one day, one year, forever? Besides he's my daddy **BUT** he killed my momma.* Although I did not have a car, the children and I took daddy many places within the neighborhood—to the park, to eat or just to watch the children play outside. Daddy was quite active and had no trouble walking anywhere he wanted to go.

Daddy had a girlfriend, Shirley, who was a very sweet lady. She would cook full course meals and invite the children and me over for Sunday dinner every week. I figured I could be nice to Ms. Shirley because she cared enough to get to know daddy after all that has gone on in his life. *I wonder what has gone on in her life for her to be understand and trusting of another human being after knowing their past; especially daddy's past.* And she is kind to my children.

22

Harvesting New Life

Remember Mr. Talk-A-Lot, Terrance? Well, we have been talking for several weeks and I really like him; he is so genuine and pure. However, there was a small issue I needed to talk over with God about him—he is seven years younger than I am. Well, I guess things can't be perfect; at least, that's what I keep telling myself. How do I get past this factor? God helped me to see that Terrance is a blessing from Him to me. It wasn't a requested blessing but one God knew I needed and maybe I was a blessing to him, too. When I first called Terrance, his mother answered the phone and she told me he was not home. So I left my name as the only message to give him when he got back home. Before his mother hung up the phone she let me know, "My son has been talking about you all week." I was taken by surprise, "Really? What has he been saying?" She continued to tell me things like, "Well, until now I thought my son had lost his mind because it took you so long to call him. He told me that he met his wife." I immediately told her, "Well, God has told him more than He has told me obviously."

Terrance and I finally spoke and I accepted his invitation to attend church with him the following Sunday. When the church service was over he introduced me to his family, church members and Pastor. I thought everyone was exceptionally nice. We spent time together at the mall while holding hands like teenagers in love. He would pick me up and take me to work every night rain, sleet or snow. He showed me pure dedication without stipulation and that was new to me. He was so very playful and even goofy sometime. I had never seen a serious side to him 'cause even then he had a smile. *Does he have a serious side?* I told him that I didn't think I was ready for a serious relationship with him or anyone else right now. But we continued to be friends.

By now, I had saved enough money to buy a car with my daddy's help while he worked seasonally and drew unemployment during in between jobs. My very own car—a Ford; it lasted for quite some time surprisingly since it wasn't brand new when I bought it. I later bought something a bit more stylish—a Mazda. The Mazda lasted many more trips back and forth to my job with the mentally ill. I have a talent working with the mentally ill. I took care of three ladies who were a real joy to me. I have had more than my share of run-ins with workers on my job who thought just because they worked with the mentally ill they did not have to treat them like they have feelings. The mentally ill bleed like people who are not mentally ill. I had finally decided to stand for holiness through my clients. On the job I had at this time, I was fortunate enough to be surrounded by workers that prayed together daily. So as we prayed together one day I had suspected inappropriate behavior taking place between a worker and a client; and while I was on my knees I asked God to have one of the clients to show signs of sickness as a sign to me that my suspicions should be acted upon. Sure enough when our prayer was over, the client was sitting up in her bed vomiting profusely. I was able to get her cleaned up and to her doctor. I explained my concerns to her doctor and he told me that I must have evidence or I would have to let my suspicions go unattended. I then prayed for my client to be sent to another home where she would be safe from further abuse. God has never let me down and He didn't let my client down either. My client was moved to a new house one month later. I started to see that God had a much deeper plan for my life. God was able to show me through my job I am able to help others spiritually without jeopardizing my job. I could actually worship God daily even in my daily activities. My life suddenly started having real meaning. Shortly after that episode I was able to find another job making even more money than before.

    I noticed so many wonderful and fulfilling instances in my life since Terrance and I met. Around Christmas time he asked me to marry him and I said yes. Being the sentimental young man that he is, Terrance wanted to replace old memories with new ones—replace bad with good. Since momma died in March we decided to get married in March so that I could have a reason to smile during that time of year. "Why not," I said. On our way to get our wedding license we noticed after we got there that we were short on cash to pay for it. *What were we going to do? Was this my sign not to do it? We have come all this way for nothing if we don't have the money.* I thought suddenly, "Terrance, go to the ATM and get more money." One of the workers informed me closing time was in ten minutes and he would never make it back in time. So another worker evidently more superior to the one speaking says, "Go ahead sir, we will wait." Terrance and I looked at other and said, "Look at God." So we planned everything and got our license to wed. It was God's will after all. We had a very small gathering at our wedding ceremony and my in-laws gave us a really nice reception at which no one really knew me at all, but they were very nice to me. Terrance and I had already been hunting for a place to live before the wedding took place but we had very little luck finding anything we liked or accommodating. Terrance's parents agreed to sign their house over to us because they had decided to move in with my husband's grandmother since she had dementia and needed round the clock care. It was as though God was putting pieces of a puzzle together and the picture was starting to make sense.

Terrance and I lived there happily for ten years with our children—Karl and Marie. After Terrance and I had been married for three years we renewed our vows and had a real church wedding since we could afford to in the beginning. It was awesome. I felt like a princess being rescued by her prince charming all over again. My daddy was able to attend our first ceremony but not the church ceremony. Daddy had gotten very sick and was unable to get around much anymore. Terrance was always supportive of me attending to my daddy's needs and never exchanged words about anything I did for daddy. Daddy had been real mild mannered until he started feeling helpless. Ms Shirley, daddy's live-in girlfriend, called me one night hysterically saying, "Your daddy has a gun on me! Please come talk to him for me." I jumped to head out there but my husband begged me not to go. I couldn't understand why after all this time he had a problem with me going to my daddy's rescue. So, he called my mother-in-law and she pleaded with me to reconsider going there myself because I could lose my life. If he's outta control she suggested I should call the police and let them handle him. So I decided not to go mainly because my wonderful husband had never interfered before and I trusted his judgment more than my own this time. The next day daddy's girlfriend left him because decided that he was not worth her losing her life.

23

Saying Good-Bye to Daddy

When daddy was sober he was a joy to be around; especially, for the children. Daddy could always find him a woman though. This time he found one with the same name as my momma's—Martha. I noticed while he was with Martha he was losing a lot of weight. He was finally admitted into the hospital because of his weight loss. I worked the third shift and would have to leave work and go straight to the hospital to be with daddy. My new pastor and his wife, Elder and Missionary Scruggs, and some of my other family members and friends were at the hospital when the doctor came in to speak with me about daddy's condition. I wanted the doctor to say everything he needed to say in front of everybody there. The doctor proceeded to discuss daddy's need for surgery but he was concerned that daddy would not survive the surgery because his heart was too weak. Daddy had cancer and it was spreading fast and there was nothing left to do. Daddy started having hallucinations of dogs in the room. I continued to reassure him that no dogs were in the room but I don't think he heard me.

Elder Scruggs explained to daddy before daddy's mind was deeply affected by the cancer that nobody could go to God for him but we must all answer to Him for ourselves. Daddy seemed to understand Elder Scruggs and the importance of clearing his communication line with God. Daddy had received all the care he could get in the hospital so his doctors assigned him hospice care. Daddy was always asking for sweets like candy and cookies; so everyday I got off work I would head to West Memphis, Arkansas from Memphis to see daddy with some goodies in hand for him. We watched TV and talked endlessly like we were trying to make up for lost time. Daddy got to the point of experiencing so much pain that he would refuse to wear his oxygen mask. So I would spend the last few hours arguing with him everyday about why he needed to keep his mask on his face. I knew he was getting tired but I couldn't let him give up like that. The doctor told me that my daddy didn't have as long as he thought but God gave him longer.

One morning after getting off work, I felt especially tired in my body so I called my pastor and asked him to check on daddy for me today. He immediately agreed. When my Elder Scruggs arrived at daddy's house he called me on the phone and said, "There is no answer at the door, so I'll just sit here in my car for a few minutes and wait around." "Okay," I replied. Shortly after our phone conversation, Ms. Martha called my phone and said that daddy just took his last breath. I let go of feelings right then that I didn't even realize I had for daddy. I loved him so much. But God loved him best. Good-Bye, Daddy, I'll miss you.

24

My Latter Will Be Greater

It has been twenty-three years since my momma's murder. Despite that fact, I can truly thank God for giving me time with my daddy before he died and for giving me time to prepare for his death instead of it being a surprise. Daddy has been dead now for three years and I sometimes think about him but I don't know whether to laugh or cry. My daddy didn't complain about his cancer or the pain that came with it he only tried to hurry its end results. He may have felt a debt to suffer. I have gone on with my life as usual. I feel like I'm living outside a shell that has just been peeled away. I am a new person because of all that I have been through. I was happy that I did all that I could do for my daddy and loved him all the way to his grave. I believed that God was pleased with me because I was obedient to His will for my life. I took care of my daddy, loved him, and gave him food, clothes, encouragement, my time and support.

Since burying daddy I have accepted my calling into the ministry as an Evangelist Missionary. I have asked God to make me over daily into the person he has intended me to be in this life. I want people to see Christ's light in me when they look at my life and to recognize that God ordains us from the beginning of time. My life has never been my own. Although, I made decisions regarding my life that were outside of God's will for me, those choices allowed me to travel right back to the road He wanted me on (I guess it was all God's road). I realize I have a ministry about love and forgiveness as I tell my life story. The two go together because in all my experiences with different hurts, disappointments, misunderstandings, persecutions and false accusations I was able to experience each of them because God put love and forgiveness inside me before I knew I would need them. I feel like retaliating sometime but I can't nail my Savior back to the cross. You see, Jesus, died so we could have a choice in whether to fight back or allow God to fight for us. I chose God to be my Warrior. I still have moments of depression but I am still under the blood of Jesus and am holding on to one day experiencing complete deliverance from all issues of my past. Until that time I will snap out of it with the help of the Holy Ghost and move on with my life.

Regardless of the hurts I continue to experience, the Lord has promised to be everything I need him to be. He was always my friend when I didn't have anyone else to depend on. When I was hurt and discouraged he comforted me daily and gave me inner peace. I have learned to accept the things I cannot change and to change only the things I can. I get up and go to work when I don't feel like it and thank God for a job to go to. I am learning to worship God in spirit and in truth. God was there for me during the murder of my mother protecting my mind and my own life when I wanted to take it from myself. Sometime I don't wanna forgive but I have learned that God forgives us over and over even before we ask for it. God has given me a new heart so that I could forgive my daddy for killing my momma; so now I'm prepared to forgive anyone for anything but God still knows the intentions of us all and has the final say on how we treat each other. God gave me back my emotions because now I care about what people do to me when at one time I didn't. I have vowed to endure what I need to in order for God to take me to the level of blessings I know he wants me to accumulate. My life is not about me but it's all about Jesus. Now that I am older I know I haven't encountered problems for nothing but to be a witness that God has a way to help us to peacefully encounter evil deeds that are done to us. To those people that said I would never amount to anything, allow me to serve notice on them right now that *I am mighty with God*. My life is filled with thoughts of pleasing God daily in my actions and my way of thinking. I must be a good example for the children that God is raising up to serve Him in His Kingdom to come.

I have arrived at the time in my life that *requires* me to share my life's story. God can bring you through the day-to-day circumstances without filling your with bitterness and hatred because those are not His attributes. We as people must learn that emotions are choices we make so why not chose to be filled with joy and let go of the weights of anger. We must be able to love our enemies and saints that are false claiming. The Bible tells us that the children of God will scarcely make it into the Kingdom of God so why should we make our chances slimmer to none by holding on to bitterness and acts of unforgiveness. My experiences have helped me to treat people the way I want to be treated and they have helped me handle situations better when people don't reciprocate acts of kindness in return. I have written this book to let you know tragedy can turn in to trilogy with God as the theme. I am a better person today emotionally, mentally, physically and spiritually (not necessarily in that order). I encourage you, Reader, to no longer allow people to dictate to you who God says that you are, but find out yourself what God says about who you are to Him. With Christ all things are possible; you see, I wrote this book when no one thought I ever could. All praises be to God, the Creator of the Heavens and Earth. I love you all!

The End

Letter to Mother

Dear Mom,

    I am writing you this letter because I will always have respect for you, the way you lived and loved. You were the virtuous woman many of us still on earth strive to become. You loved your family unconditionally by standing your ground and taking your right to love as you pleased and as it pleased God. You loved just as God desires us all to—love despite faults and to look for the good in everyone. You were so kind. You were my mom, sister and best friend. You were loved by many and now missed by all. You had the singing voice of a hummingbird. I think about you daily as I listen to the memories of you singing. I admired you because no matter how bad you were mistreated, misunderstood, abused, rejected and neglected, you still continued to love when you could have easily resorted to hate. You chose to sow good seeds and not evil—you chose life although it seems like death. You did not allow life's bitter experiences to make you transform into a bitter person but you held on to your **right** to love others. I thank God everyday for the opportunities you took to teach me early about the things you knew I would use and need as a woman to sustain myself in this world. What you deposited into me has brought me a long way. I praise God because watching you taught me to take my marriage vows seriously. I learned how to love my husband; and Mom, he loves me back. I found that real love does hurt and it comes with a price. I found myself motherless but God knew best. I remember that God promised to be everything and everybody I need Him to be—friend, mother and now a father. I can tell God secrets like I told you, momma and never have to worry about hearing them repeated or becoming distorted rumors. Because of you mom, I have found Agape Love—the love of JESUS! Thanks Mom. I love and miss you always. So until I see you again, bye for now.

Your daughter,
Lisa

Letter to Father

Dear Dad,

    I am writing to you because I loved you then and now. I just want you to know I think you were a great provider for momma and me. I realize now that you had some hard test to pass in your life and unfortunately you did not pass them all—none of us have. You made the biggest mistake of your life one day that stunted you in many ways and I still don't understand how or why you could have made some of the decisions you made but God has given me peace that. Those were YOUR decisions not MINE. I can say that **today** I thank God for the opportunity He allowed me to have in getting to know you better before He had to call you home. As God brought us together He gave me a New Heart with FORGIVENESS included inside. Forgiveness was very hard for me to learn to use but God has been patient with me as I have started to write down the instructions of how to use it in my heart. I have given up all that I knew, all that I was and all that I had to let God help me with learning to love you all over again. I'm happy that you got an opportunity to know your grandchildren. They love you Agape Style just like momma did. You attempted to explain to them various happenings of the past but I let you know it wasn't necessary because we love you anyway. You said with your mouth and I believe also with your heart that you were sorry for your actions. Daddy, I FORGIVE YOU. I appreciate you saying the words **"I'm Sorry"** because nothing could be given back to either of us. I am happy about my ability to care for you during the days of your illness; I don't regret being there for you at all but am glad that I, your flesh and blood could take care of you at such a crucial time in your life. I believe in my spirit that you had a chance to get your life in order with God. I knew this to be true when you told me as you lay there on the hospital bed that you had a "little talk with the Father" and you thanked God for giving you a daughter like me. You knew that God's spirit rests in me but you said that you must go to God for yourself. So I trust and believe that God has forgiven you and will welcome you with open arms. We love you Daddy.

Your daughter,
Lisa

About the Editor

I was born Tanya S. Lewis in Memphis, TN in 1971, and currently reside in Cordova, TN with my husband of 13 years and our five children—three sons and two daughters. Presently, I attend the University of Memphis with a double major—English with a concentration in Literature and Elementary Education. My passion for teaching children began as I learned to teach my own. With sleepless nights and countless hours at the computer learning about what interests them and ways to be creative, I have had the pleasure of learning a few things that work and things that do not.

As an active member at a local church in Memphis I have had the pleasure of exercising many of my talents and creativity. I have served as a Youth Leader, choir member, choir director, and as a Sunday school teacher. Jesus said forsake not the little children to come unto Him. As a spiritual belief I realize that I must go to God as a young child willing to open up my mind to the unknowns unafraid to make mistakes or take risks. I depend on God the same way children depend on their parents or caregivers to consider and to protect them.

About the Author

I have always known that I wanted to tell my life story and sought out the best time to do it and found it to be now in 2007. I am married with two children. My husband and I also have three godchildren that we love very much. I have worked as a CNA for many years now and have encountered so many opportunities to help people understand God's love for them. I am a Christian saved by grace and live everyday with a focus on loving others. Although I keep journals regularly jotting down experiences and thoughts as I live each day, this is my first published book. I have always found writing as a way to release bottled emotions that need somewhere positive to go. I love the art of expressing myself in a way that helps others understand their own lives better.

It is important to help others whether it is with clothing, food, wealth or camaraderie; I was taught this way. I have been known to give to others when I required at the same time but I want to live a selfless life. Charitable behavior has put me in a position to make many acquaintances. One in particular I would like to mention is my editor and friend, Tanya Mitchell. We have become best friends consistently and spiritually. I just want to thank God for allowing us to cross each other's path during this lifetime. I have already started putting future works into proposition after working together on this project.

Lisa M. Roby is a new kid on the block of authors. She has known for some time that her story had to get out—now is the time. It was in Arkansas where Lisa was born and gained her expertise and credentials to write her very own story. Lisa experienced multiple facets of abuse throughout her youth and young adult life. Cruelty was manifested in many forms—verbally, physically and emotionally. But through all the mistreatments of the juvenile Lisa, she still managed to graduate from high school and achieve a Nursing Assistant certification. Lisa Roby is now a wife and mother of two delightful children ages 20 and 16. It is clear to this new author by whom she has been ordained and predestined in order to help buff a shine on what all people today need help with... **Forgiveness**.

Lisa has taken a bold stance on the theme of Forgiveness in this invigorating non-fiction work of art. Inside she includes details of issues within her family and environment that she faced daily as a young girl that caused her to gain a personal relationship with Jesus Christ. The book tells of how she was able to endure the losses from death and the justice system.

THIS NEW AUTHOR INTRODUCES TO THE WORLD THE GROUND-BREAKING CHALLENGE OF FORGIVING ALL FAULTS OF OTHERS AS WE EXPECT GOD TO FORGIVE US

Made in the USA
Lexington, KY
06 December 2015